UNDERSTANDING MYTHS

GREEK MYTHS

NATALIE HYDE

Crabtree Publishing Company

www.crabtreebooks.com

Author: Natalie Hyde
Publishing plan research and development:
  Sean Charlebois, Reagan Miller
  Crabtree Publishing Company
Editor-in-chief: Lionel Bender
Editors: Simon Adams, Lynn Peppas
Proofreader: Wendy Scavuzzo
Project coordinator: Kathy Middleton
Photo research: Kim Richardson
Designer: Ben White
Cover design: Margaret Amy Salter
Production coordinator and Prepress technician:
  Margaret Amy Salter
Production: Kim Richardson
Print coordinator: Katherine Berti

Consultants: Noreen Doyle, M.A. Egyptology, M.A.
Nautical Archaeology, B.A. Anthropology, Art, and
Classical Civilizations: Author and consultant, Maine;
and Amy Leggett-Caldera, M.Ed., Elementary and
Middle School Education Consultant, Mississippi
State University.

Cover: A statue shows Athena protecting Schlossbrucke
(top left); the Parthenon in Athens, Greece (top right);
a painted scene showing Heracles and Athena (bottom
left); a scene showing the birth of Athena (bottom
center); a scene showing Hephaestus handing in
the new Achilles' armor to Thetis (bottom right)
Title page: Golden sculpture of Zeus

Photographs and reproductions:
Maps: Stefan Chabluk
Front cover: Wikimedia Commons: Bibi Saint-Pol: bottom (all),
Shutterstock: top (all)
The Art Archive: 5t (Palazzo Ducale Mantua/Superstock), 5b (Musée
du Louvre Paris/Collection Dagli Orti), 8–9 (Bibliothèque des Arts
Décoratifs Paris/Gianni Dagli Orti), 11 (Harper Collins Publishers),
13 (Gianni Dagli Orti), 14 (Museo Capitolino Rome/Gianni Dagli
Orti), 16b (Musée du Louvre Paris/Collection Dagli Orti), 18
(National Archaeological Museum Athens/Gianni Dagli Orti), 19
(Archaeological Museum Florence/Gianni Dagli Orti), 22 (Bardo
Museum Tunis/Gianni Dagli Orti), 38 (Museo Nazionale Taranto/
Gianni Dagli Orti). • Getty Images: (De Agostini): 24, 25, 26, 27,
30t, 29b, 33, 35, 36, 39; 29t (Photoservice Electa), 32 (Leemage), 44r
(Leemage). • The Kobal Collection: 43b (Warner Bros.). •
shutterstock.com: 1 (Nejron Photo), 4 (pandapaw), 6 (Kamira), 7
(S.Borisov), 9 (Peter Baxter), 10 (Shawn Hempel), 10–11 (Ivan
Montero Martinez), 16t (Paul Picone), 23 (Vadim Georgiev), 24
(Kamira), 30b (Elnur), 31 (NesaCera), 34t (meirion Matthias), 34b
(Olimpiu Pop), 40 (Dolgin Alexander Klimentyevich), 41 (c.), 42
(Volkov Roman), 42–43 (Antonio Abrignani), 43tl (Yuri Arcurs),
43tr (Andrey Burmakin), 44bl (Junial Enterprises), 44br (Oleg
Golovnev). • Topfoto (The Granger Collection): 12–13, 20, 37, 40–41;
(topfoto.co.uk): 15, 17 (Luisa Ricciarini), 21 (World History Archive).

This book was produced for Crabtree Publishing Company
by Bender Richardson White

Library and Archives Canada Cataloguing in Publication

Hyde, Natalie, 1963-
  Understanding Greek myths / Natalie Hyde.

(Myths understood)
Includes index.
Issued also in electronic formats.
ISBN 978-0-7787-4509-9 (bound).--ISBN 978-0-7787-4514-3 (pbk.)

  1. Mythology, Greek--Juvenile literature. 2. Greece--Religion--
Juvenile literature. I. Title. II. Series: Myths understood

BL783.H93 2012   j292.1'30938   C2011-908371-X

Library of Congress Cataloging-in-Publication Data

Hyde, Natalie, 1963-
  Understanding Greek myths / Natalie Hyde.
    p. cm. -- (Myths understood)
  Includes index.
  ISBN 978-0-7787-4509-9 (reinforced library binding : alk.
paper) -- ISBN 978-0-7787-4514-3 (pbk. : alk. paper) -- ISBN
978-1-4271-7902-9 (electronic pdf) -- ISBN 978-1-4271-8017-9
(electronic html)
1. Mythology, Greek--Juvenile literature. 2. Greece--
Religion--Juvenile literature. I. Title.

BL783.H934 2012
292.1'30938--dc23

2011050094

Crabtree Publishing Company

www.crabtreebooks.com   1-800-387-7650

Printed in Canada/012012/MA20111130

Published in Canada
Crabtree Publishing
616 Welland Ave.
St. Catharines, Ontario
L2M 5V6

Published in the United States
Crabtree Publishing
PMB 59051
350 Fifth Avenue, 59th Floor
New York, New York 10118

Published in the United Kingdom
Crabtree Publishing
Maritime House
Basin Road North, Hove
BN41 1WR

Published in Australia
Crabtree Publishing
3 Charles Street
Coburg North
VIC 3058

CONTENTS

WHAT ARE MYTHS?

People have always tried to figure out why the world is the way it is. In Ancient Greece, people looked for answers as to why Earth had hills and valleys, where different animals came from, and how humans should behave. To explain these things, they told many myths.

A myth is a narrative that often includes great heroes, **supernatural** beings, gods and goddesses, and monsters. At first, these tales were passed down from one **generation** of people to the next by word of mouth, as stories, songs, and poems. Around 2,800 years ago, the Greek alphabet was invented and the myths were written down. Some of the Greek myths we know today were found in the **epic** poems *The Iliad* and *The Odyssey*, written by a poet named Homer.

CREATION AND THE GODS

In Greek myths, forces of nature were seen as gods who had faces and names. But the gods did not live by the same rules as humans. The Greeks prayed to the gods. They built temples and held festivals to

MYTH, FABLE, OR LEGEND?

Myths, legends, and fables are all traditional stories, but each one is a little different. Legends were stories that were supposed to have taken place in history, with bits added to make them more interesting. The sinking of the city of Atlantis is a well-known Ancient Greek legend. Fables are stories told to teach us a lesson or moral. *The Boy Who Cried Wolf* is a fable, by the Greek writer Aesop, that teaches us not to **exaggerate**.

keep them happy so they would not get angry and cause disasters.

Pictures of the characters in the myths and their deeds were also used to decorate Greek vases, pots, and coins. Many famous mythical heroes and beasts were also carved into beautiful statues that decorated temples and other religious buildings. Walls were coated with plaster and painted to make **frescoes** showing the gods and goddesses at work and play. As well, small tiles of different colors were laid down in patterns to create images on the floor.

Right: The goddess Thetis gave her son Achilles his armor so that he could avenge the death of his best friend, Patroclus. (See the Achilles myth on page 21.)

Below: Nike was the winged goddess of victory and was sometimes associated with Athena, the goddess of war.

LINK TO TODAY

Many companies use names and characters from Greek myths. FTD florists use the image of Hermes, the messenger god, as a symbol of how they can deliver flowers around the world. Sports clothing company, Nike, is named after the goddess of victory, known for her speed.

ANCIENT GREECE

More than 2,500 years ago, the people of Ancient Greece developed one of the greatest civilizations **the world has ever seen. At times, the Greek** Empire **stretched from Libya in North Africa all the way to India.**

The main area of land where the Greek civilization, and later its empire, began is called Attica. It is bordered in the north by mountains and in the east, west, and south by sea. Mountains also run through the middle of the landmass and many islands dot the sea around it. These mountains and seas made it difficult to travel around Greece. As a result, each region developed its own ideas and customs. Athens became a center of art and literature, while Sparta concentrated more on military training.

PART OF HISTORY

Greeks believed that mythology was part of their history. Knowledge of different gods may have come from other cultures through travelers or merchants coming to **trade**. Gods and goddesses from different regions soon blended into the main characters that we know today.

ZEUS

In Ancient Greece, the god Zeus was called the "Father of gods and men." With his thunderbolt, he ruled over the entire universe.

Zeus's parents were Rhea and Cronus. Cronus was told that one of his children would take away his power. So he swallowed each of his children after they were born. This angered Rhea. After she gave birth to Zeus, she wrapped a heavy stone in a blanket and gave that to Cronus to swallow. She hid Zeus on the island of Crete, where he was taken care of by a **nymph** named Amalthea. The nymph hung his cradle from a tree so that he could not be found on Earth, in the heavens, or in the sea. When Zeus grew up, he used a **potion** to make Cronus cough up his brothers and sisters. They defeated Cronus and Zeus became the ruler of heaven.

MACEDONIA

Mount Olympus

Possible
site of Troy

Mount Pelion

Aegean Sea

Delphi

ATTICA

Marathon

Olympia

Athens

Ephesos

Sparta

N

Santorini

RHODES

Modern-day Greece

100 Miles

100 Kilometers

CRETE   Knossos

Above: Greece consists of a rocky
landmass and numerous islands.

Left: The Parthenon temple was
dedicated to the goddess Athena.
It stands on top of the Acropolis, or
"high city," in Athens.

CREATION AND THE GODS

There were two main types of Greek myths: creation myths and **morality** myths. Creation myths describe how the world, landscape, plants, animals, and even people came to be. Morality myths explain how people should behave and what could happen to them if they do otherwise.

One of the most common themes in Greek myths was the hero's quest. The hero must go on a journey and face terrible dangers along the way. Mythical heroes include Heracles, Perseus, and Jason.

Below: Athena (left) helped Heracles (see page 9) try to steal the sacred altar, called the Delphic Tripod, from Apollo and his sister Artemis (right).

Fate plays a big part in Greek myths. The characters go through a lot to try to change the outcome of their lives, but fail. The king of Thebes tried to avoid the **prophecy** that his son, Oedipus, would slay him. In the end, he failed and Oedipus killed him. The myths taught the Greeks that fate could not be avoided.

Lessons on how people should act were also told through myths. Goodness and **generosity** would be rewarded, but unkindness and greed would be punished. The myth of Baucis and Philemon told how they were kind to two gods disguised as ordinary people. No one else would help, so the two gods destroyed everyone in the town except the kind old couple.

Love and beauty were also found in many myths. But love did not always have a happy ending and beauty could be taken away by the gods as punishment. That was the case with Medusa, a beautiful maiden who did something wrong in a temple of Athena. The goddess punished Medusa by turning her hair into snakes and making her face so ugly, that anyone who looked at her was immediately turned to stone.

Right: In one labor, Heracles killed a bull.

HERACLES

Heracles, called Hercules by the Romans, was the son of Zeus and Alcmene. He was the greatest hero of Greek myths because of his strength, courage, and cleverness.

The goddess Hera, who was in love with Zeus, was very jealous of the child Heracles. She sent two snakes to kill him when he was a baby, but the plan failed. The boy was already strong enough to strangle them with his bare hands. Zeus wanted to protect his son. He made a deal with Hera that once Heracles was a man, he would perform 12 labors or tasks. After that, he would become a god. She agreed. She did not believe that anyone could survive the types of deeds Heracles would be sent to do. But Heracles was so powerful that he succeeded. The 12 Labors of Heracles included destroying fierce beasts, such as the nine-headed Hydra, human-eating birds, and huge, dangerous boars and bulls.

CANNIBALISM IN MYTHS!

It might seem unusual to us, but many myths include stories of people, mainly children, who were sliced, cooked, and eaten. However, the victims were sometimes coughed up whole, or rescued and put back together, as good as new.

RELIGION
AND
GODS

Many religions today believe in just one god. The Ancient Greeks followed polytheism—**they believed in many gods and goddesses. Each one had a special role in the world. Greek myths explained the origins of the gods and how they affected everyday life.**

Not all the gods had the same importance. The Greeks believed that Zeus was the king of the gods and had some control over all the others. Other gods managed certain parts of nature: Poseidon ruled over the sea, Hades ruled the underworld (where the dead were sent), and Helios ruled the Sun. Other gods and goddesses were in charge of the seasons, hunting, or music. But the gods were not seen as all-powerful. Even Zeus had to obey the Fates, who controlled what would happen in the future.

The Greek gods looked like humans and acted like them, too. They had faults and weaknesses, such as jealousy and pride and, if they did wrong, they were punished.

Greek ceremonies and **rituals** were performed at altars in temples. To keep the gods happy, Ancient Greeks made offerings and sacrifices. Animal sacrifices were a way

ORACLES

In Ancient Greece, an oracle was a person who gave good advice and could predict the future. People believed that the gods spoke directly to them through the oracle. The oracle at Apollo's beautiful temple at Delphi was a woman.

Right: This building at Delphi was used as a store house for donations to the oracle. It was built in about 500 B.C.E.

of worshiping the gods. Parts of the animal were burned for the gods, while the rest of the meat was eaten by the followers in a big feast as part of the ceremony.

Offerings were also made to different gods as a way to say thanks for blessings or to ask them for help in hard times. Food, drink, or precious items were left for the god or goddess at the altar in their temple.

Below: The Greek gods and goddesses Leto, Apollo, Artemis, and Zeus (left to right) are shown together on this carving.

APOLLO AND THE ORACLE AT DELPHI

Apollo was the son of Zeus and Leto. He had many strengths including healing, music, poetry, and archery. One of his greatest gifts was the gift of prophecy—the ability to tell the future.

In the Greek town of Delphi, lived the Python—a large snake who guarded a hole in the ground. Apollo killed the snake. The people were so grateful, they built a temple there to honor him. He decided that this was the perfect spot to share his gift of prophecy. Instead of acting as the oracle himself, he shared his gift with a priestess named Pythia. He put limits on her power, though, so she would never be as powerful as him. She could not answer "yes" or "no," but only make truthful statements. Apollo's oracle became famous across Ancient Greece for her wisdom and knowledge.

GODS OF CREATION

For Ancient Greeks, the world was created by the gods. This included not only the landscape but even the parts they could not see with their own eyes, such as the heavens and the underworld.

Through their creation myths, the Ancient Greeks were able to see the world as a place with an order to it (see the myth on page 13). Earth, love, the underworld, darkness, and night came first. In the Greek myths, these gods and goddesses, who were born at the beginning of the universe, had children who created the rest of the world. Eros was the god of love, and Nyx was the goddess of the night. Some of her children included Aether (the air), Oneiroi (dreams), and Hypnos (sleep).

(see the myth on page 13)

LINK TO TODAY

Gaia was the Earth mother and Zeus was god of the heavens. We still use the phrases "Mother Earth" and "Heavenly Father" today.

There were different classes of gods. The 12 most powerful gods, including Zeus, Hestia, and Hera, were called Olympians because they lived on Mount Olympus. They each had their own character and **domain**. They had strengths and weaknesses, and represented every part of human nature. Their relatives were the Titans, giants, and other creatures who were sent to live underground.

Left: A battle scene on a Greek vase from 570 B.C.E. shows a centaur fighting a soldier. A centaur was a mythical beast that was half man, half horse.

Above: The mythical gorgon was a terrifying woman, often with snakes in place of her hair.

CHAOS, GAIA, AND OURANOS

The Ancient Greeks believed that the gods created the heavens and Earth, and all things in them.

In the beginning, there was a vast empty space called Chaos. Out of Chaos came Gaia, which is Earth, and Eros. Gaia gave birth to Ouranos, the heavens, and she had many children with him. These included 12 Titans, who were powerful gods, three one-eyed giants called the Cyclopses, and the three Hecatoncheires, who each had 100 arms and 50 heads. Ouranos did not like any of his children, so he hid them deep inside Earth. This made Gaia angry. She convinced the Titan named Cronus to wound his father. Cronus did this and, from Ouranos's blood sprang other giants, nymphs, fierce goddesses called the Furies, and Aphrodite, the goddess of love.

MINOR GODS

The Ancient Greeks also prayed to other, less-powerful gods who roamed Earth and played a part in the everyday lives of the people. Craftworkers might pray to Techne, the spirit of art and skill. There were also nymphs, who were the spirits of Earth, sea, and sky. Dryads, who were the nymphs of the trees, were tied to their tree homes and died if the tree died.

There were also many different types of mythical beasts created by the gods. The gorgons, centaurs, Sirens, and harpies were just some of the creatures who helped or interfered with the gods, creating problems and **tension** in the world.

PROMETHEUS

Prometheus was a Titan—one of a race of powerful gods. He was the champion of humankind, and he used his cleverness to help them.

One day, Prometheus took clay and made figures of humans. The goddess Athena breathed life into the clay figures. Zeus was angry with Prometheus for creating people and refused to let him give them fire. Zeus was worried that, with fire, the humans would become powerful like the gods. But Prometheus felt sorry for the cold and hungry humans and wanted to help them. He found a reed plant with a stem filled with dry material that would burn easily. Without Zeus knowing, took it with him to Mount Olympus. He went to the place where the morning sun rose, and let the fires of the sun light the material inside the stem. He raced back down to Earth and gave fire to the humans. Zeus was so angry that he chained Prometheus to a post and punished him. Each day, a huge eagle ate his liver. Each night his liver grew back so he would be punished over and over.

Below: In one version of the myth, Prometheus modeled humans out of clay and the goddess Athena breathed on the figures to bring them to life.

HUMANS AND MORTALITY

The gods and goddesses in Greek myths were **immortal**, which meant they lived forever. They ruled their domains for all time. Unlike the gods, humans were **mortal**. The Greeks believed that, after their death, they would pass on to the underworld.

When the gods created animals, they used the help of two Titans. The Titan Epimetheus gave the animals gifts, and Prometheus inspected his work. Epimetheus gave some animals swiftness and others strength or beauty. When humans came along, Epimetheus had nothing left to give them. So Prometheus gave humans civilization and culture instead.

THE UNDERWORLD

The Ancient Greeks believed that, once thier life was over, their spirits would travel to the underworld. It was called Hades, after the god who ruled it. This place of the dead was dark and gloomy. Souls had to cross the River Acheron to reach the underworld. Charon was the ferryman who transported the souls of the dead from one side of the river to the other. Ancient Greeks placed a coin in the mouth of the dead person as payment to Charon.

Below: The Greek hero Echelos carries away the heroine Iasile to the underworld in his **chariot**, while the god Hermes leads the way.

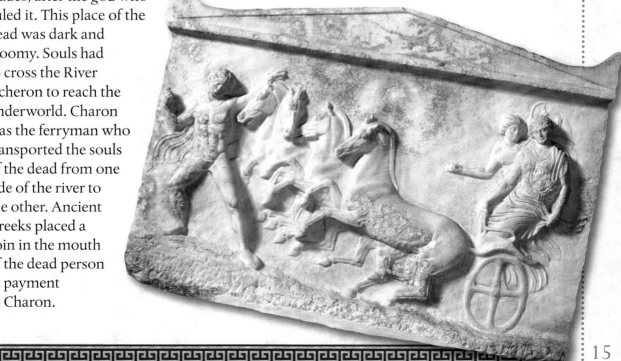

THE NATURAL WORLD

The Ancient Greeks thought that there was a supernatural explanation for the world around them. They believed that the gods shaped the land and created all the plants and creatures that lived there. Even natural disasters were thought to be the result of the actions or anger of the gods.

The majority of people living in Ancient Greece made their living by farming. They relied on the gods to provide good soil and good weather to grow and harvest their crops.

Farming was difficult in Ancient Greece. The soil was not very **fertile** and much of the land was mountainous. In the small pockets of flat land, they mainly grew olives, grapes, and grains, such as wheat and barley. With these crops, they were able to make oil, wine, and bread.

Several times a year, the people held festivals in honor of Demeter, goddess of the harvest. The people prayed to Demeter before the ground was plowed, when the grain started to sprout, and after a good harvest.

Left: Greek farmers used teams of oxen to draw a wooden plow through the ground, as in this sculpture from Ancient Greece.

DEMETER AND PERSEPHONE

The Ancient Greeks believed that the changing of the seasons and the annual cycle of growth, harvest, and rest were the result of the kidnapping and release of Persephone, Demeter's daughter.

Zeus's sister Demeter was the goddess of the harvest. When she was happy, the crops flourished. When she was upset, the crops die. The thing that made her happiest was spending time with her daughter Persephone. Persephone was very beautiful and she caught the eye of the god Hades in the underworld. One day, while she was in the meadow, he opened a great hole in the ground and kidnapped her. Demeter was heartsick. All the crops began to fail and Zeus became worried. He tried to make Hades send Persephone back. Hades refused, saying that she had eaten six **pomegranate** seeds. Everyone knew that if you ate or drank anything in the underworld, you had to stay there forever. Zeus made a deal with Hades. If Persephone married Hades, she would spend six months of the year with him in the underworld and six months on Earth with her mother Demeter. Hades agreed. While Persephone lived with her mother above ground, Demeter was happy and the seeds sprouted and the crops grew. When she returned to the underworld, Demeter cried and the plants died until Persephone returned.

A RANGE OF ROLES

Demeter was in charge of fertility, as well as harvests. Women to prayed to her to bless them with children. Demeter also became known as the goddess of marriage.

Right: This two-handled amphora or jar shows Greek farmers harvesting olives.

CHELONE

Chelone was a beautiful young nymph whose behavior resulted in her becoming the very first tortoise.

Chelone lived in a lovely home on a riverbank. When Hermes delivered an invitation to the wedding of Zeus and Hera, she ignored it. She did not want to leave her house for a silly wedding. Every guest who had been invited went, except Chelone. When Zeus found out, he was furious. He raced to Chelone's home. He threw her and her house into the river, changing her into a tortoise who would forever have to carry her house with her wherever she went.

ANIMALS AND PLANTS

The Ancient Greeks were mostly hunters and farmers, who worked closely with animals and plants in their daily lives. Many animals and plants played important roles in mythology. Myths explained how they came into existence and what special abilities each one had.

All creatures were thought to be created by the gods. Goats, bulls, and snakes were common animals in many myths. Female goats were often mother

Below: Asclepius, the Greek god of medicine, cares for an ill bedridden patient, with help from two willing assistants.

FOSSILS AND MYTHS

Researchers believe that many tales of mythical creatures actually came from ancient people finding dinosaur bones. Ancient fossil hunters measured, collected, and displayed these finds in temples. These may have been the basis for such mythical creatures as centaurs, griffons, and giants.

figures, such as the she-goat who nursed Zeus as a baby. Bulls were a symbol of strength and power, such as the bull that Heracles defeated. Snakes could be helpful or harmful in Greek myths. Snakes often protected infants or were a source of wisdom. Asclepius, Apollo's son, learned medicine by watching one serpent use herbs to bring another back to life.

Plants were seen as a symbol of life and rebirth. Often, flowers or trees sprang up where Titans, demigods, or mortals died. One Titan was **transformed** into a fig tree by his mother, Gaia.

Herbs were thought to have magical powers. They were used for charms, potions, and drugs. Some, such as aconite, were poisonous.

Right: After they were married, Melanion and Atalanta often hunted together. They killed their prey with short spears, as shown here.

ATALANTA AND MELANION

The apple was an important fruit in Greek myths. Attractive and sweet, it often symbolized love and marriage.

A beautiful princess named Atalanta was forced by her father to marry. She refused to marry, unless the man could beat her in a race. If he failed, she would kill him. A young man named Melanion fell in love with her, and he asked the goddess Aphrodite for help. The goddess gave him three golden apples, which he threw on the ground in front of Atalanta as they raced. She slowed down to pick up the apples. Melanion won the race, and he and Atalanta married.

THE UNDERWORLD

The deepest part of the underworld was called Tartarus. This was the place where sinners were punished. As his punishment for crimes against the gods, Sisyphus was forced to spend eternity rolling a heavy boulder up a steep hill in Tartarus, only to have it roll down again and have to start over.

LAND AND SEA

Myths were used to explain the **geography** of the area and its importance. When the gods created the landscape of Ancient Greece, they filled it with rugged mountains and surrounded it with a sea filled with islands.

Rivers were the homes of river gods. The most famous rivers were the five in Hades. The River Styx formed the boundary or edge between the underworld and Earth. It circled Hades nine times and had special powers. The gods swore oaths on the river. It was also the same river that the baby Achilles was dipped into to become immortal.

High places were regarded by the Greeks as sacred. Gods lived on top of mountains. Mount Olympus is the highest mountain in Greece, so this was where the oldest and most powerful gods lived.

After the gods defeated the Titans, the mountain formed and the gods moved into a palace on top of it. There was no wind, rain, or snow on this mountain and the air was pure. Many myths were based there.

Left: Charon the ferryman takes two souls across the River Styx from Earth to Hades.

AN ACHILLES' HEEL

Ancient Greeks believed that on mountains, where the gods lived, water nymphs in streams would pass on their healing whenever they touched the water. The myth of Achilles supported this belief.

Achilles was educated by the wise Chiron on Mount Pelion and grew up to be a handsome brave warrior. He was able to survive many fierce battles because of his training and also because, as an infant, his mother Thetis had dipped him into the River Styx. Every part of his body that touched the water was protected. However, his mother had held him by the heel to lower him into the water, so this heel had been left dry. Achilles died in battle when an arrow pierced his heel, the only spot where he was not immortal.

Right: Achilles was devoted to his friend Patroclus, and bandaged the wounds he received in battle. But Patroclus was mortal and soon died, while Achilles believed he himself was immortal. Today, we talk of a person's weak spot as their Achilles' heel.

Other mountains were also important in Greek myths. Mount Pelion was where the centaurs lived. One particularly wise centaur named Chiron taught some of the great Greek heroes, such as Heracles and Achilles.

NATURAL DISASTERS

With volcanoes and earthquakes in the mountains, and **tsunamis** and violent storms at sea, the Ancient Greeks had many good reasons to be afraid. Death and destruction from these natural disasters led them to believe that they were the work of angry gods.

Greece is located where Earth's **crust** or surface is fragile. Earthquakes have been felt here for thousands of years, causing monuments and buildings to fall. These were very frightening events for Ancient Greeks. Myths explained that earthquakes were the result of Poseidon, god of the sea,

Above: Here, King Odysseus and his men sail past the supernatural mermaid-like Sirens, whose songs they believed lured sailors to their deaths.

LINK TO TODAY

Plato, a Greek **philosopher**, wrote that a great civilization once existed at a place called Atlantis. He said that it had sunk beneath the water "in a single day and night of misfortune." Recent research shows that there may have been an actual natural disaster and the lost city of Atlantis did exist.

being so angry with humankind that he struck the ground with his **trident**, causing it to shake.

Often these earthquakes caused another natural disaster—tsunamis. These giant waves can form when an earthquake occurs under the sea. A wall of water comes rushing ashore, sweeping everyone and everything away. To calm Poseidon, Ancient Greeks made offerings to him, usually sacrificing a bull or an ox. Sailors often made offerings and said prayers to Poseidon before beginning a trip to sea, asking him to keep the waters calm and smooth.

The hecatoncheires were three giants who were responsible for violent storms or hurricanes. They were given homes in deep rivers or the sea, and, allowed storms to brew when the gods called for them.

The active and extinct volcanoes have created many of the islands in the sea surrounding Greece. In about 1600 B.C.E., a volcanic eruption on the island of Santorini wiped out a colony of Minoans, who were a highly advanced civilization at that time.

POSEIDON AND TYPHON

Storms, earthquakes, and volcanic eruptions were only some of the punishments that angry gods inflicted on humans.

Poseidon and two of his brothers, Zeus and Hades, decided to divide the world between them, each taking one third. Zeus was to rule the heavens, Hades the underworld, and Poseidon the seas. Poseidon had a temper and was quick to get angry and seek revenge. When sailors did not respect him, he sent storms and caused shipwrecks and drownings. He was also able to make Earth shake violently when he was upset, causing earthquakes. Zeus was challenged by Typhon, the son of Gaia and Tartarus. Typhon was a fierce creature who had snakes for legs and dragon heads instead of fingers. He tried to defeat Zeus to become ruler of gods and mortals. But Zeus used a flash of lightning to conquer and imprison him under Mount Etna. There Typhon still rages with anger, causing boiling fire to come out of the mountain and throwing fiery rocks into the sky.

Left: Poseidon, the Greek god of the seas, known to the Ancient Romans as Neptune, is usually shown holding a three-pronged trident.

DAILY LIFE

Ancient Greece was made up of many small city-states. Each was called a *polis* and usually consisted of a single city, protected by walls, and the countryside around it. The Greeks took great pride in their culture, arts, and government.

Each polis was run by its citizens, who not only took part in **politics** but were expected to serve in the army, work as officials, and volunteer for **jury** duty. Not everyone could be a citizen. Greek society was made up of two main groups: free men and their families, and slaves.

BUYING ONE'S FREEDOM

Sometimes slaves were able to buy their freedom with money they may have saved or borrowed. If a master agreed to this, the slave would have to pay an amount equal to their value if they were sold. Some of this money was often used as an offering to a god such as Apollo. Once free, the slaves mostly had the same rights as metics (see page 25) but could never become citizens.

Above: This Minoan fresco shows a fisherman holding his catch of fish, ready to be sold in the market and eaten by the master and his slaves.

Free men could own property and had legal rights, while slaves had nothing. Many slaves lived closely with their owners, but they were hardly ever granted their freedom.

Even being a free man did not guarantee citizenship. In Athens, only free men who were born in the city could become citizens. Those who were born in another polis but came to live in Athens were called *metics*. Metics paid tax and served in the army, but they could not own property or participate in politics.

Most citizens had at least one slave and several servants. They modeled their society on that of the gods. In Greek myths, slaves and servants often played important roles. When the great hero Heracles killed a king, he was punished by being made a slave. One year, he was slave to Queen Omphale of Lydia, and even had to dress like a woman and do women's chores.

Right: Slaves did many menial tasks around the house, such as grating cheese.

LINK TO TODAY

You can see the Ancient Greek word *polis* appear as the root of many modern words, such as metropolis (a large, urban center), police (a group that enforces the law), and policy (procedures used by a government).

ERICHTHONIUS

The people of Athens were proud to say that they could trace their kings back to Gaia, the Earth mother. They also believed that the gods founded and protected their city and gave them knowledge.

Gaia was the mother of Erichthonius, but he was raised by the goddess Athena. When he grew up, he took over the throne and became king of Athens. While king, he taught Athenians how to till the earth with a plow, how to smelt silver, and how to yoke horses to pull chariots. He used to race chariots. Zeus was so impressed with his skill that when Erichthonius died, Zeus raised him into the heavens to become the group of stars known as the charioteer.

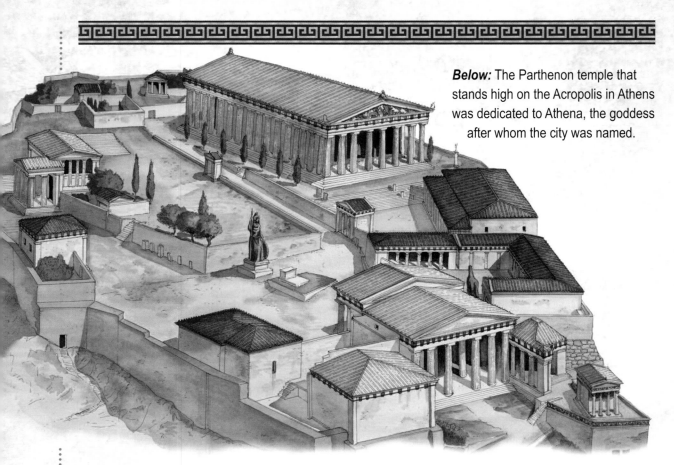

CITY-STATES, OR *POLEIS*

The different poleis of Ancient Greece were often **rivals** and fought wars against one another. Although they were independent from one another, they still shared a common culture, language, and religion.

Two of the major city-states in Ancient Greece were Athens and Sparta. Athens was the largest and richest polis. Athens was a city of culture and was filled with beautiful buildings, artworks, and sculptures. Many of the famous poets, artists, and thinkers came from Athens.

Just as the gods and goddesses built their palace high up on a mountain, the Acropolis, or "high city," in Athens was built on a rocky hill. Large beautiful

NAMING ATHENS

Greeks believed that Athens got its name as a result of a contest between Poseidon and Athena. Both wanted the city named after them. They agreed that they would each give a gift to the people and let them decide. Athena's gift of an olive tree was the best, so the city was named Athens in her honor.

temples on top of it honored Athena, the goddess who gave her name to the city.

In Sparta, the Ancient Greeks focused less on the arts and more on warfare. Spartans were known as fierce warriors.

They valued good health and exercise for men, women, and children. This prepared the men to be strong and brave soldiers, and helped the women to have healthy babies who would become soldiers when they grew up.

The Spartans did not believe in comfort or beauty of any sort, so there are very few ruins of temples or buildings from this area. The Spartans, like the Athenians, traced their kings back to the gods through myths. Their first king was a son of Zeus and married a woman named Sparta, whose great-grandfather was Poseidon.

PANDORA'S BOX

Hephaestus, the god of fire, was ordered by Zeus to make a woman out of clay. Hephaestus created a beautiful woman named Pandora. Her failings were said to be the reason there was so much trouble and war among humankind.

Zeus gave a locked box to Pandora and told her to never open it and look inside. Pandora tried very hard not to open the box, but it looked so mysterious that her curiosity grew and grew. Finally, one day, she opened the box. Out flew all sorts of troubles and miseries— sickness, greed, hatred, anger, despair, and cruelty were now out in the world to cause grief for humankind. She closed the lid as quickly as she could, trapping only hopelessness inside, so humankind at least still had hope in their world.

Left: In the myth, Pandora, a young woman much like this figure, opened a locked box given to her by Zeus and released many troubles into the world.

FAMILY LIFE

The roles of men and women in Greek society **reflected** the roles of gods and goddesses in mythology. The main male gods ruled the sky, underworld, the seas, the Sun, and medicine. The goddesses were concerned with home, harvest, and love, and protected marriage and young girls.

In Ancient Greece, men were the head of the family, just as Zeus was the head of the gods. Men did not spend a lot of time at home. They were busy running the government, managing their farms, or taking trips for business. People who moved from town to town looked up to Hermes, the god of travelers. Traders prayed to Poseidon to grant calm seas for their merchant ships. Soldiers called upon Ares, the god of war, to give them strength and courage in battle.

Women ran the household and did not often leave their homes. Their lives revolved around the family, meals, and raising children. Hestia, the goddess of the hearth, was so important to women that nearly every house had in their courtyard an altar dedicated to her. Women prayed to the goddess Aphrodite about matters of love and to Hera as the protector of marriage.

Children were a blessing in Greek families. Only boys were educated in school because they would be the next citizens and soldiers. They learned reading, writing, and recited poetry about the gods.

HESTIA

One of the most important goddesses to women was Hestia. There was an altar to Hestia in every house and offerings were made to her for harmony in the home.

Hestia was the first child born to Rhea and Cronus, and the first to be swallowed by him. When Cronus began to cough up his children, she was the last to appear. She was then called both the oldest and the youngest of his children. The gods Apollo and Poseidon, wanted to marry her. She swore by Zeus, her brother, that she would never marry. Hearing this, Zeus told her that if this was her wish, then she would forever stay on Mount Olympus. She became known as the heart of the home. The hearth in every home was an altar to Hestia. She taught the women how to cook bread and make the family meal. Hestia never left her home on Mount Olympus, and never got involved in the problems or struggles of men.

NEWBORN CHILDREN

Before a newborn child could be accepted into the family, it had to be carried around the altar to Hestia, the hearth, while prayers were said to the gentle goddess.

Girls were educated at home. They learned to read and write only if their mother could teach them. They were taught to honor Hestia and could also count on Athena, the goddess of wisdom and weaving, to help them with the skills they would need to run a successful household when they grew up.

Right: One educated woman was the poet Sappho, who was born on the island of Lesbos around 620 B.C.E. Little of her poetry survives.

Below: The women of Ancient Greece did not often leave their homes and had to make their own entertainment.

29

FESTIVALS AND ENTERTAINMENT

Greek society included time for fun and relaxation. People went to festivals, theaters, and sporting events, and enjoyed parties at friends' houses. The gods were part of all these joyful celebrations.

Nearly all festivals in Ancient Greece were in honor of a god or goddess. People often paraded through the streets to the temple, where they offered prayers and sacrifices to the god. The Thesmophoria Festival, celebrated only by women, took place in the fall. It included a nighttime torch-lighting ceremony to remember Demeter's torchlight search for her daughter Persephone. Many festivals honored the god Dionysus (see page 31) and included drinking contests.

The Greeks enjoyed plays and concerts. Almost every town had its own theater, where plays were held as contests. The best **playwright** would win a prize of an ivy wreath. The two types of plays, tragedies and comedies, often showed the gods and humans together.

Above: There were more than 200 different dances in Ancient Greece. Some dances were warlike, while others were suitable for weddings or funerals.

LINK TO TODAY

The Muses were the goddesses of music, dance, literature, theater, history, and astronomy. Melpomene was the Muse of tragedy and Thalia the Muse of comedy. These two opposite figures are often shown today as frowning and smiling masks.

THE BIRTH OF DIONYSUS

Ancient Greeks enjoyed festivals and entertaining. Wine and wild behavior were seen as gifts from Dionysus.

Dionysus was born the son of Zeus and a mortal woman named Semele. Zeus was so happy she was going to have his child, that he granted her a wish. She asked that he come to her in his true form as a god. Zeus begged her to change her mind, but she was determined. Zeus's true form was a thunderbolt and so he burned her. Luckily, she survived. Dionysus was sent to be raised by nymphs and educated by the god Hermes. The nymphs taught him how to grow grapes and make wine, so he became the god of wine and the giver of joy.

ORPHEUS

Orpheus was the greatest musician. When he played his songs on his lyre, an early stringed instrument, there was a magical effect on everyone and everything around him.

Jason was an adventurer who was about to set out on a sea voyage to find the mythical Golden Fleece. He asked Orpheus to go along with him. Orpheus was a great help along the way. When the sailors were frightened, Orpheus would play a soft melody that would calm them. When they were tired, he would play a song to give them the energy to continue. But most importantly, he helped them pass the Sirens safely. The Sirens were beautiful creatures who were half woman and half bird. When they sang, sailors became enchanted and crashed their boats onto the rocks and drowned. When the Sirens began to sing, Orpheus played his own tune and Jason and his men were able to sail past the rocks safely.

Right: Greek jockeys rode bareback on their horses, as shown in this ancient bronze figure.

PELOPS

The Ancient Greeks prized the spirit of competition. In the myth of Pelops, his chariot race is one of the origins of the Olympic Games.

Pelops fell in love with the princess, Hippodamia, as soon as he saw her. But her father, the king of Pisa, did not want her to marry. He challenged Pelops to a chariot race. If Pelops won, he could marry Hippodamia. If he lost, the king would kill him. Pelops went to the god Poseidon for help. Poseidon gave him horses from the god Ares. But the king of Pisa had a magic chariot. Before the race, Pelops had someone loosen the wheels on the king's chariot. During the race, the king's chariot crashed and killed him. Pelops won the race and married Hippodamia, and ruled Pisa with her for many years.

THE OLYMPIC GAMES

One of the most famous sporting events held today has its roots in Ancient Greece. Ancient Greeks believed that the Olympic Games were first created by the hero Heracles, or by King Pelops, to honor their victories in contests (see pages 9 and 32).

Ancient Greeks began competing in sports and held the first Olympic Games in 776 B.C.E. Athletes had to be citizens of certain city-states to compete. The three original events of the games were running, wrestling, and chariot racing.

They symbolized the gods' mythical activities and were associated with skills needed for war. They were part of Greek soldiers' training. In one type of footrace, men wore armor just as soldiers did going into battle. This helped them build up their strength, stamina, and running speed. Different types of chariot races were held, including one with mules. Wrestling competitions were inspired by myths, such as Heracles wrestling the giant Antaios.

The *pankration* was a special event in honor of the myth of Theseus fighting the **minotaur**. It was a combination of boxing and wrestling, and was very dangerous. In the *pentathlon*, athletes competed in five events: running, jumping, wrestling, hurling the discus, and throwing the javelin. These involved skills that soldiers needed to cover a lot of ground, throw spears, and hurl rocks. The Olympic Games were held every four years in Ancient Greece. During the event, poets, artists, and sculptors would showcase their skills. Prizes were given for the best. A huge gold and ivory statue of the god Zeus was placed in the main temple. It became one of the Seven Wonders of the Ancient World, but was destroyed in the 4th century C.E.

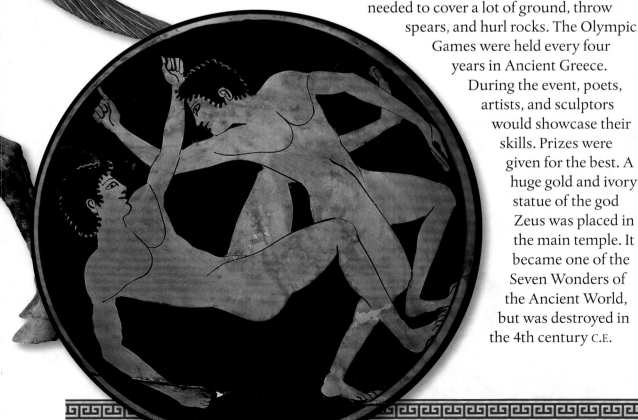

Below: Wrestling was one of the three original events of the Olympic Games, along with running and chariot racing.

TRADE *AND* WARFARE

The Ancient Greeks looked to their gods to help them in trade and conquests. They traveled by land and sea to many different places around Greece. Trade was vital to the Greeks because their poor farmland meant they could not grow enough food for all their citizens. Armies traveled to expand the empire through warfare.

The heart of every Ancient Greek city was its main square, called an *agora*. This was used as a place to meet, and to buy and sell goods. Shopkeepers sold their products and farmers sold their produce. To pay for these goods, each city issued its own coins.

Below: The agora or main square in Athens was often packed with people buying and selling goods or just talking with their friends.

HERMES

From an early age, Hermes, the god of trade, was good at making deals.

When Hermes was a child, he found a tortoise shell. Stretching strings across it, he made it into a lyre. He was able to play the lyre so beautifully that, when the god Apollo heard it, he offered to trade Hermes his cows for it. Hermes accepted the trade, but as Apollo was getting the cows ready, Hermes made a pipe and began to play it. The music was so wonderful, that Apollo wanted the pipe as well. He offered, Hermes the golden staff he used to herd the cows. Hermes did not accept so quickly this time. He told Apollo that, as well as the staff, he wanted his gift of prophecy so he could tell the future. Apollo could not refuse and traded Hermes the golden staff for his knowledge of prophecy.

Coins from Athens showed an owl, a symbol of the goddess Athena. Other cities decorated their coins with images of gods, such as Poseidon, or dolphins, for Apollo.

Greece did most trading with other countries by sea because it was surrounded on three sides by water. Merchants traded with port cities around the Mediterranean Sea and north into the Black Sea. They traded such products as pottery, wine, and oil for goods such as grain, silver, gold, and ivory. As they traveled, they spread the Greeks' belief in their gods far and wide.

The Greek trading ships had one square sail, so they depended on the right winds to carry them across the water. Sailors worshiped the winds as gods, who also had names and personalities. The four main wind gods were Boreas (north wind), Zephyrus (west), Notus (south), and Eurus (east). These gods could be gentle, like the west wind, or fierce, like the north wind that brought icy **gales**.

Below: Most Greek boats had one square sail. But some, like this one, were powered by oars.

THE TROJAN WAR

The story of the Trojan War is one of the most famous Greek myths of all. It was described in two epic poems—*The Iliad* and *The Odyssey*—written by Homer in around 750 B.C.E. These texts are two of the oldest surviving stories of the gods and goddesses of Ancient Greece.

The war between Greece and Troy—in what is now Turkey—began as a fight over a princess. Zeus arranged for his daughter, Helen, to marry King Menelaus of Sparta. She, however, fell in love with Paris—the son of King Priam of Troy. Helen ran away with Paris back to Troy.

The Greeks were furious and demanded that she return. When she did not, they marched to Troy and fought for 10 years to capture the city and bring back Helen.

Above: During the Trojan War, Patroclus, a friend of the Greek hero Achilles, was killed by the Trojans. Achilles then killed many Trojans in response.

To capture the city and win the war, the Greeks had to trick the Trojans. This they did successfully (see myth on page 37).

Knowing that there had been a real war around 1250 B.C.E., some people wondered if this myth was based on true events. In the 1870s C.E., a German **archaeologist** named Heinrich Schliemann set out to find the ruins of the city of Troy. Following Homer's description, he started to dig in Turkey and found the remains of a city that had been destroyed in a war. Researchers now believe that there was an ancient city of Troy, just as Homer described it.

THE TROJAN HORSE

The Trojan Horse was the brilliant idea of King Odysseus. With this clever trick, the Greeks finally found a way into the city of Troy to end the Trojan War.

The city of Troy was so well protected, the Greek army could not get inside the city walls. The Greeks decided on a daring plan. Odysseus, a Greek king famous for his cleverness, had a dream that told him what to do. With the help of Athena, goddess of warfare and wisdom, the Greeks built an enormous horse out of wood. They hid their bravest soldiers, including Odysseus, inside the horse. The Greeks left the horse at the walls of Troy, while the rest of their army sailed away. The Trojans took the horse into the city, and argued about whether to destroy it. They decided to leave it as an offering to their gods. The Greek soldiers emerged from their hiding place during the night, defeated the Trojans, and brought an end to the war.

Right: The Trojan Horse is shown on this storage jar found on the island of Mykonos. This jar is 2,600 years old.

LINK TO TODAY

The saying "Beware of Greeks bearing gifts" refers to the story of the Trojan Horse. People still use this saying today as a way to remind people to be cautious of unexpected gifts.

Above: Alexander was a great horseman, riding his favorite horse Bucephalas in sport and into battle for more than 20 years.

ALEXANDER THE GREAT

Alexander was the son of King Philip II of Macedon. Macedon, now called Macedonia, is a separate country just north of Greece. When Alexander became king in 336 B.C.E., he formed a huge army and conquered Greece, and much of Asia. By the time he died, he was known as Alexander the Great.

As a boy, Alexander was taught by the philosopher Aristotle . Aristotle had lived most of his life in Greece and loved the Greek way of life. He taught Alexander everything he knew about Greek myths, history, and thought.

THE GREEK WORLD

Although not Greek himself, Alexander spoke Greek and believed in the Greek gods. He modeled himself after Achilles and was taught to ride, hunt, and fight. After his father Philip died, Alexander enlarged the territory ruled by the Macedonian kingdom. He conquered many different countries and cultures, including Egypt and Persia. Wherever he went, he introduced Greek writing, music, dance, myths, money, art, medicine, and theater.

Even when these distant countries were later conquered by new armies, Greek myths and ideas remained. When the Roman Empire grew strong during the second and first centuries B.C.E., Greek myths survived, although the gods were given new names: Zeus became Jupiter, Poseidon became Neptune, and Ares was now Mars.

Right: Alexander would have fought his many battles with a sword like this. The blade is made of bronze and the hilt is gold.

ALEXANDER'S MOTHER

Alexander's mother Olympias said, that the night before her wedding, she dreamed that a thunderbolt had entered her body. She took this as a sign that Alexander's father was actually Zeus. She believed her son was part god and directly related to the great heroes Achilles and Heracles.

THE GORDIAN KNOT

Ancient Greeks believed that the right to be king was a gift from the gods. The gods often gave humans a sign to watch out for so they would know the right person was taking the throne.

The people of Phrygia had no king, but the oracle said that their king would arrive by oxcart. One day, a man named Gordius came into Phrygia on an oxcart, so the people made him king. Gordius was so grateful that he dedicated his cart to the god Zeus. He tied the cart up with a very complicated knot and left it in the temple. The oracle said that Zeus was pleased and that anyone who could untie the knot would be ruler of all Asia. But the knot was so tricky to untie, that it stayed knotted for many generations. When Alexander the Great invaded Asia, he came upon the cart and the knot. He believed that he was destined to be ruler and could most certainly untie the knot. After trying for some time and becoming frustrated, Alexander drew his sword and sliced through the knot and untied it. Alexander went on to create one of the largest empires in ancient history.

GREEK LEGACY

The myths of Ancient Greece still have an impact on our society today. These myths have shaped our ideas about architecture, sculpture, poetry, theater, science, medicine, math, law, and government, among other things.

The temples that the Greeks built for their gods were carefully balanced in size and shape. Their height and length resulted in the right number of columns so the temple was not only a strong structure, but was also pleasing to look at. These temples have been copied in buildings all around the world. The Brandenburg Gate in Berlin, Germany, and the Capitol Building in Washington, DC both use an Ancient Greek style in their design.

Most Greek sculptures tell the stories of gods, mythical creatures, heroes, and monsters. They also showed the human body in amazing detail. Even today, carved scenes on flat slabs of stone, called *reliefs*, as well as statues are influenced by Ancient Greek art. The Golden Boy statue on the top of the Manitoba Legislative Building in Winnipeg, Manitoba, is an image of the Greek god Hermes.

Epic poems are long narrative tales of heroic deeds. They were first written by the Greeks. The most famous are *The Iliad* and *The Odyssey* (see page 36). This style of writing is found in such recent epic poems as *Evangeline: A Tale of Acadie*, written by Henry Wadsworth Longfellow in 1847 C.E. It is about the Acadian people being driven out of the Maritime area of Canada and sent back to France.

All movies and plays that we watch today had their beginnings in the theaters of Ancient Greece. The first plays were part of festivals to the gods, during which stories were acted out on stage. The use of costumes, masks, and even special effects were all inventions of the Ancient Greeks.

Left: The 17th-century C.E. French artist Claude Lorrain painted this Ancient Greek scene of Apollo and the Muses.

Below: This statue of the Greek god Eros stands in the center of London, England.

THE MUSES

The nine Muses were daughters of Zeus who lived on Mount Olympus. They were the goddesses of writing, music, and dance, and the inspiration for poets and playwrights. They made such sweet music together that, when they sang, the heavens and Earth all stopped to listen.

A nearby king had nine daughters who thought their talent was just as good as the Muses. They challenged the Muses to a contest, with the nymphs as judges. The nine sisters went first and sang their song. Then the Muses sang. Without hesitation, the nymphs declared the Muses the winners. The nine sisters began to squawk and complain about the result, until the Muses had enough. They turned the sisters into chattering birds called magpies.

LINK TO TODAY

Eros, god of love, is often shown carrying a bow with which he fires love arrows or love darts. A person who suddenly falls in love is said to be "love struck" by such an arrow.

NEMESIS

Nemesis was the goddess of retribution, punishing people for their evil deeds. She watched human happenings and would step in to right any wrongs.

One day Nemesis saw Narcissus, who was very handsome but also very vain, sitting by a pool of water. A beautiful nymph named Echo took one look at Narcissus and fell in love with him. But Narcissus had no time to be kind to her and she eventually faded away until only the sound of her voice remained. Nemesis punished him by making him fall in love with himself. He spent so much time staring at his reflection in the water that he wasted away and became the narcissus flower that grows near the water's edge.

ASTROLOGICAL ZODIAC

The 12 constellations of the zodiac can all trace their meanings back to Greek mythology. The twins of Gemini, who were Zeus's sons Castor and Pollux, Leo the lion, who was killed by Heracles as one of his 12 labors, and Scorpio the scorpion, who killed Orion, were all Greek mythological figures.

SCIENCE AND MEDICINE

Ancient Greek beliefs in the role of the gods in science and medicine still affect how we understand and use these skills today.

If you look up into the night sky, you might see groups of stars called *constellations*. Many of these groups are named after Greek gods or creatures. In Greek myths, Orion was a hunter who boasted that, with his dog Sirius, he would kill all the creatures on Earth. The goddess Artemis, who wanted to protect the animals, sent a scorpion to kill him, As the constellations of Orion and Sirius move across the sky, they are chased by the constellation of Scorpio.

The Greeks thought the healer Asclepius was so skilled that he could bring the dead back to life. This angered Zeus, who killed him. After Asclepius died, he became the god of healing. People built Ascelpions or shrines that usually included a temple, hospital, gardens, and gymnasiums. Modern health clubs are very similar to them.

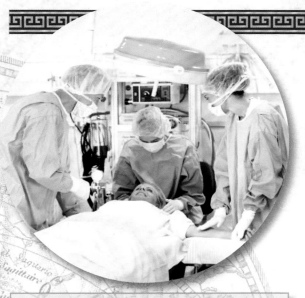

HIPPOCRATIC OATH

Doctors swear the Hippocratic Oath today to say they will practice good medicine. The oath was written by the Ancient Greek doctor Hippocrates. He may have been the first person to put forward the idea that diseases were caused by something natural and were not punishments from the gods.

GEOMETRY

Geometry is the branch of math concerned with lines, angles, surfaces, and solids. Greek mathematicians, such as Pythagoras and Euclid, proved the rules of geometry were true. Euclid's book *Elements* was used to teach geometry for more than 2,000 years and we learn Pythagoras's theorem today.

THE FATHER OF SCIENCE

Thales of Miletus is often called the "Father of Science." He was an Ancient Greek philosopher who tried to describe the world in natural rather than supernatural terms. He looked to science and math as a way to explain the shape of Earth, the movement of stars, and even electricity.

Left: Movies about the Trojan War and other events from Ancient Greece are very popular today.

LAW AND DEMOCRACY

Just as gods gave out punishments and rewards for people's behavior in the myths, the Greeks did the same in their courts. They were the first people to use a jury to help decide the guilt or innocence of an **accused** person. Jury members were picked at random at the last minute, and there could be more than 200 for each trial. This large number was chosen to make it too difficult for the accused person to bribe or threaten them all and wrongly win his or her freedom.

In the democracy of Athens, each year, 500 men were chosen from the citizens of Athens to serve as lawmakers for one year. The rest of the citizens would each have one vote on any laws these men passed, and majority ruled. This system of involving as many people as practical in decision-making is the basis of our modern democracy today.

Right: The Greek goddess Dike holds the scales of justice, weighing the case for and against the accused person.

OSTRACIZED!

The Greeks used a special system known as **ostracism** to get rid of a politician or other unpopular person. Citizens wrote down the name of the person on pieces of broken pottery called *ostraka*. If 6,000 votes against him were collected, he had 10 days to leave the country for 10 years, or face death.

Left: Pieces of *ostraka,* or broken pottery, found on the Acropolis in Athens.

LINK TO TODAY

We can trace our modern alphabet back to the Ancient Greeks. Although they got the idea to write things down from their trading partners, the Phoenicians, the Greeks added symbols for vowels—something no other written language had before. Symbols for vowels and consonants created words.

TIME CHART

3000 B.C.E. The first settlement on the Acropolis is built in Athens

2600 B.C.E. Minoan palaces are built on the island of Crete, including one at Knossos, believed to be the home of King Minos; an underground labyrinth houses the minotaur

1700 B.C.E. Palace of Knossos is destroyed during an invasion

1600 B.C.E. Volcanic eruption on Santorini wipes out Minoan civilization

1250 B.C.E. Trojan War begins

1240 B.C.E. The Greeks use the Trojan Horse to defeat Troy

800 B.C.E. Greek alphabet developed

776 B.C.E. First Olympic Games are held

750 B.C.E. Homer composes, or writes, *The Iliad* and *The Odyssey*

594 B.C.E. Solon introduces many reforms in Athens and lays the foundations for democracy

510 B.C.E. Democracy is introduced by Cleisthenes, who becomes known as the "Father of Athenian Democracy"

497 B.C.E. Persian Wars begins; the Persians outnumber the Greeks, but the Athenians have a swift navy and the Spartans have a fierce army

490 B.C.E. The Greeks defeat the Persians at the Battle of Marathon

449 B.C.E. The Persian Wars end

447 B.C.E. Construction of the Parthenon begins—a temple to the goddess Athena on the Acropolis in Athens

446 B.C.E. A 30-year peace treaty is signed between Athens and Sparta

430 B.C.E. The plague kills about one-third of all Athenians

420 B.C.E. Construction of the temple of Athena Nike at the Acropolis

399 B.C.E. Trial and execution of the philosopher Socrates for corrupting the minds of the youth of Athens

380 B.C.E. Plato establishes the Athens Academy on the site of a sacred grove of olive trees dedicated to Athena, the goddess of wisdom

359 B.C.E. Philip II becomes king of Macedon (now Macedonia) and begins to expand his empire

336 B.C.E. Philip II is assassinated; Alexander the Great becomes king

323 B.C.E. Death of Alexander the Great at age 32

146 B.C.E. The Romans invade Greece and govern the country, adopting the Greek gods and giving them new names

[Note: Some historians give slightly different dates for these ancient events]

GLOSSARY

accused Charged with or put on trial for a crime

archaeologist A person who studies ancient human life and remains

chariot A two-wheeled cart pulled by horses

civilization A very developed and organized society with cities

crust The solid outer shell of Earth

dedicated Devoted to, used to honor something

domain An area or territory

empire A group of states or countries under one ruler

epic Lengthy or grand; an epic is a very long poem

exaggerate To talk of something as being bigger, greater, better, or worse than it really is

Fate A supernatural force that decides events outside of a person's control

fertile Healthy and able to grow crops

frescoes Paintings done on wet plaster

gale A very strong wind

generation All the people who are roughly the same age

generosity Being kind and giving

geography The physical features of Earth

immortal Able to live forever

jury Group of people who hear a law case and make a judgment

minotaur A Greek mythical creature that is half man and half bull

morality Good human behavior

mortal Will eventually die

nymph A female spirit of nature

ostracism The act of voting to send someone unpopular away

philosopher A wise person who tries to explain and interpret ideas

playwright A person who writes plays

politics Activities having to do with government

polytheism A belief in more than one god

pomegranate An orange-sized fruit with sweet flesh and many seeds

potion A liquid with healing or magical properties

prophecy A prediction of what will happen in the future

reflected Looked and/or behaved the same way as something or someone else

rituals Set patterns of actions related to a custom or tradition

rivals People competing against one another

supernatural Belonging to forces outside of the laws of nature

tension Strain or pressure

trade The process of buying and selling goods or services

transformed Changed dramatically

trident A spear with three prongs

tsunami A long high wave caused by an earthquake under the sea

LEARNING MORE

BOOKS

Amery, Heather, and Linda Edwards. *Greek Myths for Young Children.*
London: Usborne, 1999.

Chrisp, Peter. *Ancient Greece,* New York: Dorling Kindersley, 2006.

D'Aulaire, Ingri d'Aulaire and Edgar Parin. *D'Aulaires, Book of Greek Myths.*
New York: Delacorte Books for Young Readers, 1992.

Green, Jen. *Hail! Ancient Greeks.* St. Catharines, ON:
Crabtree Publishing, 2011.

Osborne, Mary Pope, and Troy Howell. *Favorite Greek Myths.*
New York: Scholastic, 1989.

Peppas, Lynn. *Life in Ancient Greece.*
St. Catharines, ON: Crabtree Publishing, 2011.

Powell, Dr. Anton, and Sean Sheehan. *Ancient Greece.* Revised edition.
New York: Facts on file, 2003.

WEBSITES

Ancient Greece: The British Museum
www.ancientgreece.co.uk/

Greek myths for kids
www.historyforkids.org/learn/greeks/religion/greekrelig.htm

Greek myths
http://storynory.com/category/educational-and-entertaining-stories/greek-myths/

Greek mythology for kids
http://greece.mrdonn.org/myths.html
www.mythweb.com/

Greek myths, legends, gods
http://atschool.eduweb.co.uk/carolrb/greek/greek1.html

Greek gods and goddesses
www.greek-gods.info/greek-gods/

[Website addresses correct at time of writing—they can change.]

INDEX